Blairsville Junior High School
Blairsville, Pennsylvania

Design David West

Editor Steve Parker

Researcher Cecilia Weston-Baker

Illustrator Aziz Khan

© Aladdin Books Ltd 1988

Designed and produced by
Aladdin Books Ltd
70 Old Compton Street
London W1

*First published in the
United States in 1988 by*
Franklin Watts
387 Park Avenue South
New York NY 10016

ISBN 0-531-10625-X

Library of Congress Catalog
Number: 88-50495

Printed in Belgium

Contents

UNDERSTANDING DRUGS

AIDS
AND DRUGS

Nicholas Bevan

FRANKLIN WATTS
New York · London · Toronto · Sydney

INTRODUCTION

What are the facts on AIDS? After all the news and publicity in recent years, you might think that people now know all about this illness. Not so.

"Well, it's a disease that gays catch, isn't it?"

"How? . . . gay sex, I suppose . . . "

"Straights only catch AIDS if they do it with lots of people, and don't use condoms."

"There's a treatment now to cure AIDS."

None of these "facts" is true. AIDS does not affect only gays (homosexuals), but straights (heterosexuals) too, and bisexuals, drug injectors, babies...in fact almost anyone. Particular groups of people do not matter so much. It is more the sorts of behavior an individual follows. "High-risk" types of behavior increase the chances of AIDS.

We cannot cure AIDS. Millions of people all over the world will die from it. But we can act to slow its spread by changing our behavior, to limit the possibility of catching the virus (the "germ") that causes the disease.

The main link between AIDS and drug abuse is the needle and syringe used for injecting drugs. The "AIDS virus," HIV, lives in blood and certain body fluids. If someone with AIDS has used a needle or syringe then these items could well carry the AIDS virus. If they are

Drug-abuser's dilemma: AIDS and drugs make a mighty problem.

5

shared, the next user might catch it. Friends, parents and agencies, as well as the AIDS victims themselves, are struggling to deal with new and very complex problems.

One lesson from the latest research is that drug injection is increasingly important in the spread of AIDS. It can provide a way for the disease to gain a foothold in the general population. It could happen like this:

Several men take drugs, and they regularly share their needles and equipment (their "works"). A newcomer with a cheap supply of drugs joins their group. He has HIV, the AIDS virus. He doesn't know it, and neither do they. They share "works." As a result, one of the group catches the virus. Later, he makes love to his girlfriend. They have been faithful to each other for a few years, and they see no point in using a condom. He passes HIV to her during sex. After a while, their relationship breaks up. AIDS takes a long time to make itself known, and she still does not realize she has the virus. She meets a new boyfriend, and eventually they make love. Perhaps he has never had sex before and never used drugs. But now he has HIV, and he'll probably develop AIDS.

❝ AIDS . . . will test our fundamental values and measure the moral strength of our cultures. World Health Organization official. ❞

AIDS AND DRUG ABUSE

" *I only use my own needle. I always used to share with my mates, but I don't share at all now.* "

AIDS stands for Acquired Immune Deficiency Syndrome. This disease is caused by a tiny "germ" called HIV, the Human Immunodeficiency Virus.

The details about AIDS – exactly what it is, how it spreads, and what it does to the body – are explained later in the book. Here are some of the main facts.

HIV, sometimes called the AIDS virus, can only be caught in certain ways. One is during "unsafe sex." Another is by using a needle and syringe that has already been used by someone with the virus, and that has not been sterilized.

People who have HIV in their bodies, but who don't yet show any signs of illness, are called HIV positive. HIV may remain undetected for years; the person may look and feel quite healthy. When the virus becomes more active and starts to cause ill health, we say that the person is developing AIDS itself, often called *full-blown AIDS*. So far, no one who has developed full-blown AIDS has recovered or been cured. A very high proportion of people infected with HIV are likely to develop full-blown AIDS (see page 25).

Drug abuse and AIDS
Drug abuse and AIDS together make a mighty problem. People who inject themselves with illegal drugs have enough troubles already. There may be difficulties that drove them to drug abuse in the first place. Since drugs are no answer, they probably still have these difficulties. They could be caught by the law, and fined or put in prison. They

Staring AIDS in the face: a doctor examines a sufferer.

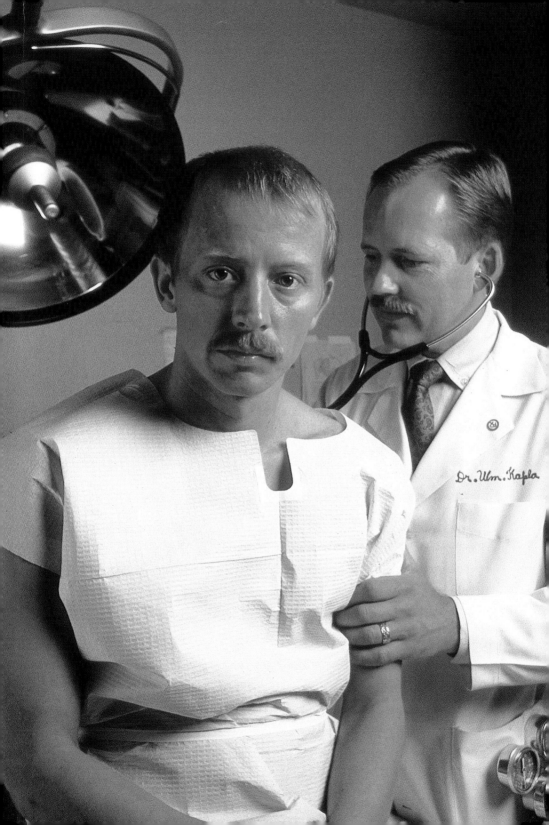

may have problems with money and in holding down a job. Or they could be out of work and stealing to get money to buy drugs. They may have no friends and be shunned by their family. The drugs they take have bad effects on their bodies and minds. Catching AIDS is just another risk . . . there are so many risks already, what's the difference?

But there's a world of difference. With the right help and advice, then coming off a drug, or problems with money, or the law, or getting a job, could be sorted out. There's always a chance of going back, of somehow making a fresh start. But with AIDS, as far as we know, there's no going back.

How drug abuse spreads AIDS

You can't catch the disease from some forms of drug abuse, such as drinking too much alcohol, or snorting cocaine, or getting high on speed pills. At least, not unless you run other risks associated with catching AIDS.

❝ Basic hygiene is the answer to the virus – it is caught by sharing needles, not cups.
Scottish AIDS Counselor. ❞

People who inject drugs are the ones most at risk. HIV lives in blood and body fluids. Each time a person uses a needle and syringe, a tiny trace of blood is left inside. If he or she is infected with HIV, the blood may contain viruses. If someone else uses the needle or syringe, that drop of blood gets mixed up with the drug preparation. The next user is, in effect, injecting that trace of blood into his or her body. It doesn't matter how small the amount is. A drop of blood too small to be noticed can contain thousands of viruses. What is important is that sharing a needle with someone who is infected with HIV means that there is a risk the needle could be contaminated with the virus, and if so, there is a risk of injecting HIV. It does not matter how "clean" the needle or syringe looks on the outside.

The increase in drug injectors with AIDS has been dramatic.

AIDS and drug abuse

The numbers of people who inject drugs and have AIDS is increasing fast. In some European countries, 4 out of 5 cases of AIDS are in intravenous drug injectors. The figures below come from a 24-country survey.

1984 1 per cent increase

1985 7 per cent increase

1986 14 per cent increase

1987 16 per cent increase (preliminary)

There's always a first time

The greater the quantity of infected blood that gets into someone, the more chance there is of catching HIV. And the more a needle is shared, the greater the risk of infection. Sharing the needle transfers blood from one person to another, and traces of every user's blood are left behind. So it is the act of sharing a needle, rather than how often you take drugs, that creates the risk.

But with AIDS, once is enough. You don't have to be a drug addict, or even an occasional user. People have

❝ *Free needles will support the drug community, but arrest AIDS spread.* *Health Worker.* ❞

caught HIV the first time they ever used a needle. One teenage girl described how she worried a lot before trying a drug for the first time. Would she like its effects so much that she would want more? Could she become an addict? These are risks of drug abuse, and they are dangerous enough. However, what she didn't consider was that sharing a needle could give her AIDS. It did, and she died.

Risk-free needles

There needn't be the risk of catching AIDS from a needle. Thousands of people have injections every day – as part of the medical treatment for diseases, such as diabetes, or in hospital, or at the dentist, or when donating blood. Ear-piercing, tattooing and acupuncture also involve sticking

Posters on a New York street warn of needle-sharing dangers.

needles into the body. A few cases of AIDS may have been transmitted in this way.

But there is no risk of AIDS if the needles, syringes and other equipment are perfectly *sterile*. This means they have been specially treated, by radiation or heat or chemicals, to kill all the germs on and in them. They are stored in germ-free containers, which are only opened just before they are used.

Doctors, nurses and others are supplied with sterile needles and syringes. A fresh set every time. The equipment is destroyed after use, so that there is no chance of it being reused. Then, if someone infected with HIV has an injection, there is no risk of the virus being passed on.

Risks with needles

So why do injecting drug users use someone else's "works" – their needle, or syringe, or mixing equipment – which may contain HIV? What makes them take such an enormous risk with life?

Some have ingenious excuses. One addict said that he read about the problem in a magazine. The article referred to *intravenous* drug users – those who inject directly into a vein. He didn't do this; he "popped" his drug just under the skin. Yet the problem is not how or where you inject, into a vein or muscle or under the skin, but simply that you inject. Whatever the type of injection, it may transfer HIV if infected blood is in the needle or syringe.

When questioned again, the addict admitted he really knew this. He was trying to delude himself.

❝ *I share needles only with people I know well.* ❞

The ritual of sharing

Needle-sharing can be a kind of ritual which some drug users find satisfying. It gives them a sense of belonging, of being one of the crowd. Drug addicts are often shunned by society, and they may have few friends or nowhere to live. Getting together to share their drugs and equipment is one way of feeling wanted. But the risk of injecting AIDS is so real. Set against it are the feelings of wanting to be part of a group. Some injectors say they share only with people they know well, who wouldn't have HIV. But no one can tell, by looking, whether a person has the virus.

The need for a "fix"

Some drug abusers are so "hooked" that they do not care what they use to inject. Their whole life revolves around getting their next "fix." They may lie, cheat, steal and kill for their addiction. Most experts believe heroin is the worst drug in this respect. For some addicts, the chance of catching AIDS seems less important than missing the next fix.

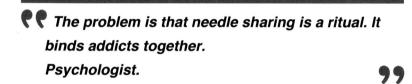 **The problem is that needle sharing is a ritual. It binds addicts together.**
Psychologist. **"**

AIDS and the general population

In July 1987, the U.S. Public Health Service published figures for various groups of people who carried HIV. They estimated that up to one and a half million Americans are

Sharing a needle can bind the group, like passing around tobacco.

infected. Homosexuals are still the largest overall group. But in New York City, drug injectors are the fastest-growing group. They make up one HIV carrier in three, and this proportion is rising. Overall, in the United States, about one drug addict in six is infected with HIV.

The figures also showed that about four babies out of five born with HIV, were born to a mother who was a drug abuser infected by HIV.

AIDS is already spreading among drug injectors in Europe. In Edinburgh, Scotland, more than half of injecting drug abusers are infected with HIV.

Another great danger is that AIDS is finding its way, via drug abusers, into the millions of people in the general

population. In the early days, AIDS was largely limited to homosexuals – and mainly to those homosexuals who had a large number of partners. Then some hemophiliacs were infected. Now drug injectors are the growing group.

Experts say that drug abuse is the most common way that HIV reaches the heterosexual community. Needle sharing is the "bridge." A drug user with HIV shares a needle, and passes on the virus to the sharer. The sharer then lends the needle to someone else, and passes on HIV. He or she also has unsafe sex, and passes it on this way. It is easy to see how AIDS spreads so fast.

Drugs change hands, and with them, the threat of injecting AIDS.

A question of risks

Should we have advertisements and publicity about safer, but still illegal, ways to inject drugs – in the same way we've had adverts for "safe sex?" Could publicity encourage people to try drugs?

No kind of drug abuse is without risks. There's no such thing as "safe" drug abuse. The publicity is aimed at making a very risky business just that little bit less risky. The only way to be really safe is to avoid drugs altogether.

Research by the New York Public Health Department indicates that some drug injectors see AIDS as a new and frightening way of dying, compared to other risks, such as overdose. Hopefully this is making them change their ways.

New needles for old

What about "needle exchanges?" In most areas of the United States, a prescription is required to obtain a syringe and needle legally. Would "needle exchange" programs encourage drug abuse and make it easier to be an addict? It is not clear. Yet most doctors and researchers feel that the danger of AIDS and its spread is greater than the danger of drug abuse.

In some places, new needles for old are only given on condition that the drug abuser attends for treatment or counseling, to try and stop taking drugs. In some drug advice centers, this has caused arguments and violence, with attacks on staff. Several experts say that anyone should be able to exchange a needle, whether or not they are trying to be "cured" of their addiction.

WHAT IS AIDS?

" It's the sneakiest virus of all. It goes for the crucial link in the immune system, the cells at the heart of the fightback effort. "

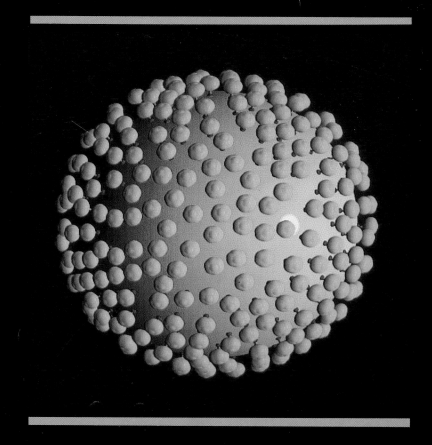

AIDS is a new disease. It was first described in the United States in 1981. Previously fit people were suddenly becoming ill with very rare diseases. The diseases were normally seen only in those who had a damaged *immune system* – the system in the body that defends it against germs and fights off illness.

The disease was Acquired, which meant it was "caught" and not inherited from parents. It affected the Immune system, making it Deficient (damaged and unable to work properly). And it showed itself as a Syndrome – a group of illnesses, which could occur singly or together, with many possible symptoms. So the new disease was named Acquired Immune Deficiency Syndrome: AIDS.

❝ *The cell manufactures and releases a whole new generation of viruses before it dies.*
New Scientist *magazine.* ❞

Illnesses that AIDS brings

In AIDS, the body's immune system cannot battle against illness and destroy invading germs. This means that people with AIDS are more likely to get illnesses which they would normally be able to fight off with little trouble.

Many people with AIDS develop forms of cancer. One of these is Kaposi's sarcoma, sore-looking spots and patches on the skin. The surface of the skin becomes blistered and purplish blotches occur.

They may also have serious lung conditions such as pneumocystic pneumonia which affect breathing.

AIDS may affect the digestive system, so that food is not used efficiently by the body. The person loses weight and suffers chronic diarrhea. Gradually the body wastes away because of lack of nourishment.

The disease may also attack the brain and the spinal cord, causing loss of memory and odd behavior.

The lymph nodes get bigger. These are the "glands" that swell during an ordinary infection, in the neck, under the arms, and in the groin. In AIDS they become very enlarged, in a condition called *lymphadenopathy*.

These are some of the problems that AIDS can bring. A sufferer becomes more ill as different diseases take hold. The body cannot recover, and finally gives up the fight.

The AIDS virus

AIDS is caused by Human Immunodeficiency Virus, a microscopic "germ." Many other diseases, such as flu and measles, are caused by viruses. There is a different kind of virus for each disease. Actually, AIDS is not caused by "a virus." There's not just one. A tiny speck of blood can contain numerous HIVs.

The body's immune system is our protection against viruses, bacteria and other germs. It develops an attack force called *antibodies*, tiny chemical substances in the blood and body tissues that fight the invaders. But HIV is a sneaky infiltrator. The immune system detects it, and produces antibodies, in the usual way. But HIV is unusual because it knocks out parts of the immune system. And it converts immune cells to work for it, producing more viruses.

HIV, the AIDS virus

The photograph on the right shows HIVs "budding" from a host cell, magnified 200,000 times. One entire virus is only one-tenth of one-thousandth of one millimeter across. If you lumped together 1,000,000,000 (one billion) viruses you might just be able to see them as a tiny speck.

In order to survive, a virus must get into a living cell. This cell is called the host. Once inside, the virus "hijacks" the cell and sets it to work, making copies of itself. The cell dies in the process, and the viruses within are set free.

HIV infects only humans. To begin with, its host cells are a special type of white blood cell called T4 lymphocytes. Once attacked, the host lymphocytes are turned into HIV factories. The new HIVs are released from their hosts. They travel to new host cells in other parts of the body, infect them, multiply again . . . and so AIDS takes a hold.

How HIV multiplies

T cell's infected genes

Lymphocyte T cell's genetic "factory"

HIV genetic material

New HIVs

HIV

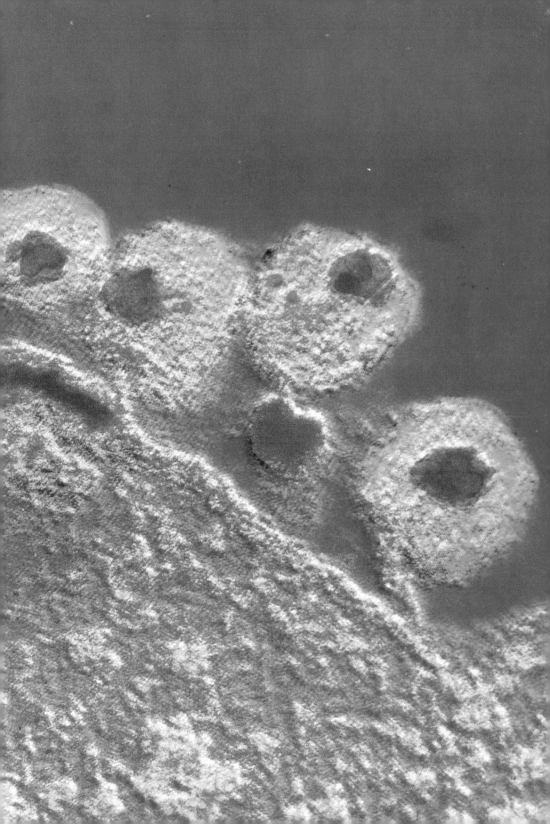

like itself. In the end, they destroy the body's defenses.

Infection

When a person catches HIV, the "AIDS virus," that person does not yet have AIDS.

When a virus gets into someone's body, we say that the person is *infected*. One great problem with HIV is that it may live in the body for several years, without causing any problems. This time, while the virus is "sleeping," is called the *incubation period*. During it, the person is *contagious* or infectious. He or she probably shows no outward signs of illness. But a blood test would show that the person is HIV positive. Studies indicate that how infectious a person with HIV is varies with time. Also, the resistance to becoming infected with HIV may vary.

❝ *It's the sneakiest virus of all. It goes for the crucial link in the immune system, the cells at the heart of the fightback effort.* **❞**

Full-blown AIDS

Being HIV positive does not mean that a person has AIDS. The person becomes ill. Now he or she has what's known as *full-blown AIDS*. We might say that the person "has AIDS." People with AIDS die from a whole variety of other illnesses that AIDS lets in. Many are infections, like pneumonia. They are called *opportunistic infections*, since they seize the opportunity to infect while the immune system is damaged.

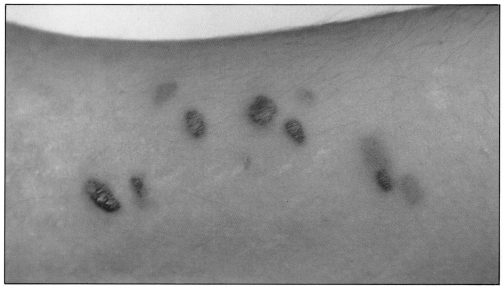

Kaposi's sarcoma, an early sign of AIDS in some people.

How many HIV carriers develop full-blown AIDS? In 1985 the figure was as low as 1 in 20. Newer statistics from various studies suggested it might be more than half. Now, scientists believe that almost all people infected with HIV will eventually develop AIDS.

What happens to AIDS patients?

In countries such as Britain, AIDS patients who become very ill are cared for in hospital until they die. Some regions have special wards to care for people with AIDS, giving them care and counseling. In certain cases, just a few minutes spent talking to patients reveals the agonies they go through, and how they wished they had taken more care.

Some people with AIDS have helped to warn other people about the illness. They talk to groups, appear in videos and leaflets, and generally try to inform people of the dangers. They want to pass on the messages about safe sex and not sharing needles and syringes. This takes tremendous courage.

Special risks for drug users

For drug users the risks of catching HIV are as follows:

● *Low risk – taking drugs by means other than by injection; injecting but only with your own equipment which is never ever shared; sharing limited to one partner when both partners have not shared with anyone else or had sex with anyone else for many years; sharing, but always fully sterilizing the equipment between uses.*

● *Medium risk – sharing with a small group of friends (see page 14); sharing very limited, equipment cleaned effectively between each use.*

● *High risk – frequent sharing of equipment with others; sharing with a casual group of friends, some of whom share outside the original group; sharing with anyone at any time.*

THE ORIGINS OF AIDS

❝ The 80s will go down as the decade that AIDS began. We want to know - why? ❞

Where did AIDS come from?

No one knows for sure where in the world, or exactly when, the HIV virus begain to infect people, or when AIDS itself began. It may have been in more than one place at the same time. It is possible we shall never know.

Scientists have studied viruses similar to HIV that are found in monkeys and apes. It is a possibility that one of these changed and came to infect humans, although again how this could have happened is unclear.

Some scientists have suggested that AIDS began in Africa. It may have then spread to Haiti and the Caribbean, and then on to the United States and so to Europe. "Gay jet-setters" may have been one link. Another could be the colonial links between some African and European countries. However the pattern of the world spread of AIDS has not been studied in enough detail as yet.

The story may go back further than 1981, when AIDS was first recognized in the United States. Blood stored in Zaire in 1959 has been examined, and contains HIV. So possibly the virus has been around for many years, at least in Africa. In 1988 it was discovered that a 16-year-old boy, who died in the United States in 1969, probably had AIDS. After his death, doctors saved frozen samples of his blood and tissues, since they did not recognize his unusual illness. Recent tests show he had HIV. There may be similar isolated cases. However, for some reason, AIDS only began to take hold and show itself in the 1980s. It may be that the generally good level of "background" health in the United States allowed the virus to be recognized.

AIDS in the United States

The Center for Disease Control in Atlanta estimates that there are probably 1.5 million people in the United States who are infected with the AIDS virus now. They also figure that approximately 180,000 of these will die of AIDS by 1991. Drug injectors are the fast-growing group.

The World Health Organization says that more than 50,000 people have full-blown AIDS. These are certain cases, from countries that test for AIDS. There are many thousands more people from poor countries who have AIDS. But their doctors and hospitals do not have the resources even to test for the virus, let alone care for the victims. They are struggling against many other diseases, like malaria and typhoid.

Over the next 20 years, AIDS will kill millions of people around the world. In parts of Central Africa, its effects may be greater than anywhere else. Here, it is common among the general population in some urban areas.

💬 *AIDS seemed so far away from our small town. Now two people here've got it. We're all scared stiff. Who's next? How'll we know?* 💬

AIDS in the UK

In Britain at the end of July 1987, there were 906 reported AIDS cases and 529 deaths. It is thought that by 1990 there will be 10,000 people with AIDS, and 100,000 positive for HIV. If the British pattern follows the American one, drug injectors will be the fastest-growing group.

Pregnant women queue for AIDS tests in an African hospital.

How the virus spreads . . .

HIV is quite fragile, for a virus. Away from the human body, it becomes ineffective. It cannot spread in many of the ways we usually imagine we "catch" an illness, such as shaking hands or drinking from the same cup.

However, HIV thrives in blood and certain body fluids. It is the mixing of body fluid from a person infected with HIV, with that from someone who is not infected, which creates the risk of HIV being transferred from the former to the latter person.

Mixing of blood or body fluids from two people (one with HIV) can therefore transmit AIDS. Body fluids mix during sex, and blood mixes if drug injectors share needles or syringes.

Guys in Times Square: the gay community has responded to the AIDS threat.

... Through pregnancy

The child of a mother with HIV is at risk of catching the virus. During pregnancy, the blood supplies of the baby and mother are closely linked, and HIV may pass across. And at birth, the blood of mother and baby may mix.

There have been several hundred babies born with AIDS in the United States. Only a few cases have been reported in Britain. But in Africa the problem is gigantic. In Zambia, doctors fear that almost 6,000 babies with HIV were born in 1987. Most infected children die before the age of five years.

... By blood transfusions and blood products

Hemophiliacs suffer from an inherited disease in which

blood does not clot to seal a cut or wound. They need regular transfusions of a special blood preparation, or they may bleed to death. The blood is donated by other people.

In the past, some people with HIV have given blood. This contaminated blood (or part of it) has been passed on to hemophiliacs, who in turn became infected with HIV. This is now impossible in the United States, since all donated blood is tested for antibodies to HIV. Also, people wishing to donate blood are asked not to do so if they are in one of the high-risk AIDS groups. In most Western countries there is a similar system.

How AIDS is *not* spread
These are ways you cannot catch AIDS:
- *by shaking or holding hands*
- *from door handles or toilet seats*
- *by everyday close contact such as holding, cuddling, stroking and caressing*
- *by sharing cups or cutlery*
- *from insect bites*
- *from clothes*
- *from bathroom items*
- *from ordinary kissing*

AIDS AND SEX

❝ AIDS *seemed so far away from our small town. Now two people here've got it. We're all scared stiff. Who's next? How'll we know?* **❞**

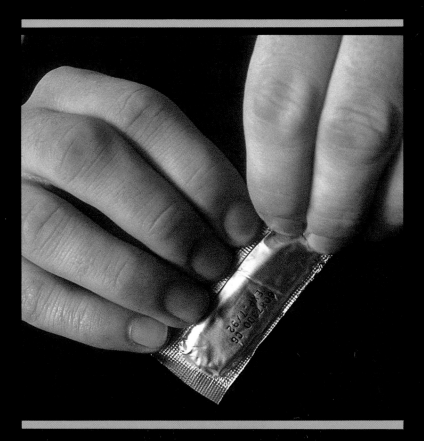

In many forms of sex body fluids, where the AIDS virus lives, may mix. This includes vaginal sex, when the man inserts his penis into the woman's vagina, and anal sex, where it is put into the anus, and oral sex, where it is put into the mouth.

There are two main questions. One: could a partner have HIV? Two: which type of sex is least likely to pass on the virus – what is "safe sex?"

Who carries HIV?

You cannot tell by looking at someone if he or she has HIV. Anyway, they may not know themselves. But, on average, certain groups of people are more likely to be infected. If you are considering sex, you should consider the risks.

In a close relationship, it is far better to get things out in the open and talk frankly about AIDS, rather than worry on your own in silence. And remember, you are never alone.

These babies have the AIDS virus. For them, life will be short.

Advisors and counselors are available to help you, in complete confidence. Also, what might your partner be thinking? Could he or she have the same worries about you?

In general, the greater the number of sexual partners a person has, the greater the chance that he or she carries HIV. Once a man carries HIV, he can pass it on to a woman during vaginal intercourse. She can then pass it on to another man. If he is bisexual, he can pass it to other men and women. There is a saying, in terms of AIDS, that when you sleep with someone, you are in effect sleeping with all their partners over the past five years. If you have any doubts, get some advice from a qualified person and talk it over with your partner.

Prostitutes are a very high-risk group. Not only do they have sex often, with many different partners, but some of them also inject drugs.

What is "safe sex?"
Using a condom (a prophylactic sheath or rubber) can greatly reduce the chance of passing on the virus. The condom must be used according to the instructions on the packet. Condoms were designed to act as a barrier to sperm, so that pregnancy cannot happen. They also act as a barrier to HIV, for both partners.

There are several aspects to "safe sex." One is your partner – could he or she have the AIDS virus? Another is the type of sex you have. And another is using a condom properly.

AIDS and sex: risk factors

These are the chances of catching HIV during sex, if the partner already has the virus:

● *No risk – caressing or masturbating by oneself.*

● *Very low risk – dry kissing (lips lightly on lips or skin), mutual masturbation.*

● *Maybe risky – wet, deep kissing, especially if one partner has bleeding gums or mouth ulcers.*

● *Probably risky – oral sex.*

● *Medium risk – vaginal intercourse with a condom, risk increasing if condom is not used correctly, such as putting it on over the tip of the penis only.*

● *High risk – vaginal intercourse without a condom, or with several sexual partners, or sharing sex toys such as vibrators.*

● *Extremely risky – anal intercourse, condomless vaginal intercourse with prostitutes.*

● *The element of risk increases with the number of sexual partners you have.*

❝ **We all saw the ads for safe sex. My friends didn't seem to bother. I wasn't sure, I wanted to be careful, but not to be laughed at for being a wimp.** ❞

Safe . . . or safer?

It has long been known that using condoms as contraceptives, for birth control, is not 100 per cent effective. Most experts agree that condoms have a "failure rate" of about

10 to 15 per cent. This means if 100 couples use this method of birth control, on average about 10 to 15 of the women are likely to become pregnant. There are various reasons, including condoms not being put on correctly, or slipping off, or becoming damaged during sex.

No "park bench" risk: normal social contact does not spread AIDS.

Using a condom with a spermicide reduces the failure rate to about 5 per cent. A spermicide is a special cream or other preparation that kills sperm.

Some experts say that, as with birth control, condoms have a "failure rate" when used to prevent the spread of HIV. Condoms greatly reduce the risk of transferring the virus to one partner, if the other partner has it. But they do not give total protection. It is important that people understand there is still a risk of HIV being transferred, even with a condom. Perhaps the term should be "safer" sex rather than "safe" sex.

Some condoms are coated with a spermicide containing a chemical (such as nonoxyl 9) that kills HIV. These should be more effective that the type of condom designed mainly for birth control.

Strains on the relationship

❝ The hard sell for safe sex appears to curtail the spread of AIDS in the gay community, especially with anal sex. There is no comparative action for needle users.
Doctor. ❞

The shadow of AIDS has fallen over many relationships. One couple described how, before AIDS, they did not mind if their partner had sex with someone else occasionally. They had an "open relationship ." However, the possibility of HIV infection during sex with someone else had changed things. The man wanted to continue having occasional sex with other women, while taking great precautions against catching HIV. The woman disagreed. She preferred to take no chances – which meant occasional sex with others was

The shrink-packed condom: a vital weapon in the AIDS war.

out for her, and for him.

After several arguments, the couple split up. Some months later the man returned. He said he had changed his mind, he now agreed with her, and he wanted to get back together. He said he had not had sex in the meantime. But the woman could not convince herself that he was telling the truth. She said that she still loved him, but she "loved herself" more. She was not prepared to put her life at risk. She thought that AIDS had "driven a wedge" between them. Their relationship was over.

❝ I loved him, and wanted him. But, with him, there was a definite chance of catching AIDS. I finally decided I couldn't take that chance. ❞

MEDICAL DRUGS FOR AIDS

"Although we are reasonably hopeful, we do not want to give false hopes. Daniel Zagury, AIDS researcher, Paris."

Viruses are not usually affected by medical drugs. Diseases caused by bacteria can be treated with *antibiotic* drugs such as penicillin. But antibiotics don't work against viruses. A virus uses host cells to multiply. To stop this happening, a medical drug would have to harm the host cells – which are the body's own cells.

> **Although we are reasonably hopeful, we do not want to give false hopes.**
> **Daniel Zagury, AIDS researcher, Paris.**

A cure for AIDS?

Medical researchers have been trying to develop *antiviral* drugs for many years. These would work against viruses, like antibiotics work against bacteria. AIDS has given their research new importance, and work is going on around the world. But there are many difficulties, including the way the virus multiplies. Workers must have strict germ-free conditions, so that they do not pick up HIV themselves. Despite the efforts, most experts agree that a medical drug to cure AIDS is still some years away.

A vaccine for AIDS?

When we are babies, we receive "jabs" – injections of a *vaccine* that contains dead or ineffective germs. We do not become ill, but our immune systems react by making antibodies just as in a real infection. Then, if live germs try to infect the body, the immune system can beat them off before they multiply. This process is called immunization.

Could we find a vaccine against AIDS that would immunize the body against this disease? Again, researchers around the world are trying to find the answer. But it's a lengthy business, requiring tests in the lab, on animals and then on selected people. Tests take several years to make sure there are no long-term bad effects.

If a vaccine for AIDS is discovered, could we wipe it out? This is a long way in the future. Some scientists feel it will be several years, perhaps 20 or more, before a vaccine is developed. Even when they find one, money will be needed to produce it on a massive scale and distribute it to millions of people around the world.

Treating AIDS

At present, AIDS cannot be cured or prevented. Can it be treated? To an extent, yes. One company makes a medical

Under the microscope, infected immune cells carry their deadly HIV cargo.

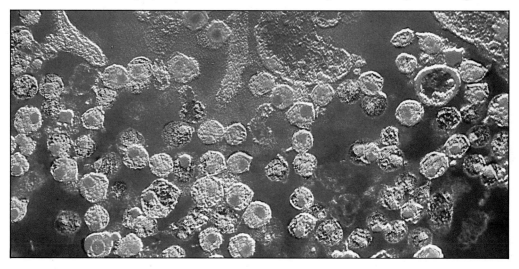

drug called retrovir zidovudine, also known as azidothymidine or AZT. This can have side effects. But in some people with AIDS it is thought AZT has delayed its progression, for a time. In one study, someone with AIDS and without AZT had a half-and-half chance of living for another year. With AZT, the chance was up to nine-in-ten. AZT does not stop carriers from passing on the virus. Neither does it protect others against infection. Several other medical drugs are being tested in the hope of finding a treatment. One is peptide T, which may stop HIV from identifying its host cell. Another possible is dideoxycytidine, a drug related to AZT, one of the nucleoside group. Also on the researchers' lists are the interferons, natural body chemicals that have been tried against other viral diseases and cancers.

❝ I hope that there will come a day when no new drug is considered newsworthy.
Samuel Broder, National Cancer Institute. ❞

Alternating therapy

Some people with HIV have been treated by "alternating therapy." This means giving them one drug for a time, then swapping to another, and back to the first, and so on. This gives the body time to recover from the side effects of one drug while on the other, yet the anti-HIV action continues non-stop. For example, AZT can cause anemia – lack of healthy red cells in the blood, which means oxygen is not

Preparing AZT, a medical drug that slows the progression of AIDS.

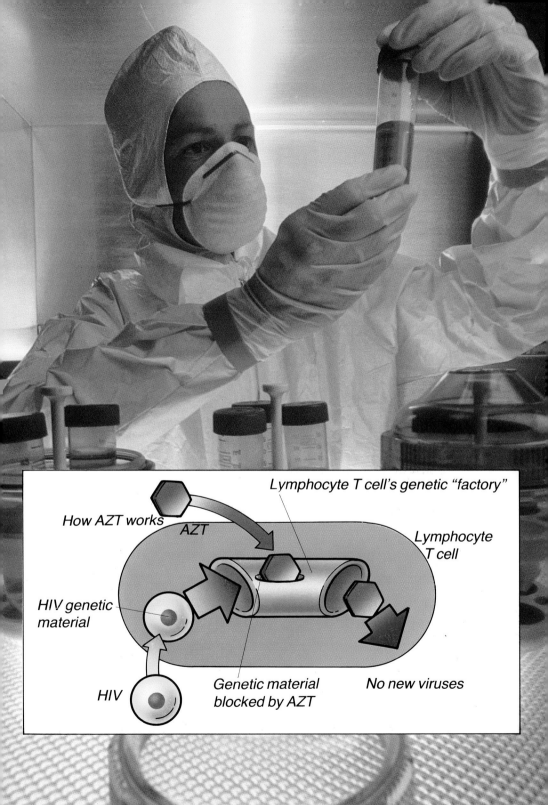

How AZT works

AZT

Lymphocyte T cell's genetic "factory"

Lymphocyte T cell

HIV genetic material

Genetic material blocked by AZT

HIV

No new viruses

carried around the body efficiently. Dideoxycytidine can cause pains in the legs and feet. By giving these two alternately, side effects can be "stopped before they start."

One patient in the United States took AZT and dideoxycytidine alternately for about a year, and did not suffer from side effects. Some researchers and doctors think it likely that alternating therapy, and medical drug "cocktails" combining two or more drugs, will be developed that should improve on today's treatments.

Across the world, millions of people are hoping that the medical researchers win. Those with HIV infection would benefit from better treatment or a cure. Other people wait for a vaccine that could protect them against AIDS. In 1979 the World Health Organization officially declared that the terrible disease of smallpox had been wiped out, after a long, worldwide campaign. Can AIDS be beaten, like smallpox? There is unlikely to be a "miracle cure" for AIDS in the next year or two. But most scientists are hopeful that it can be beaten – and sooner, rather than later.

❝ *Curable? No. Treatable? To a limited extent. Preventable? By a vaccine, no – but by changing our behavior, yes. This is how we must fight AIDS.* **❞**

IF YOU'RE WORRIED

"Prevention is better than cure. And when there's no cure, prevention is all we have."

It is important to remember that AIDS is still a relatively uncommon disease in Europe and the United States. There are several reasons why we seem to hear so much about it: it's a new disease, it is fatal, and it is spreading so fast. Drug abuse is one of the main ways in which it spreads.

How to avoid AIDS

A basic way to avoid catching HIV is to be aware that some life-styles make HIV infection more likely . Remember that after someone becomes infected, it often takes many years (up to eight or more) before signs of full-blown AIDS appear.

The spread of the virus can be contained or controlled by avoiding certain types of known high-risk behavior. Of course, they cannot take into account each person's situation. You may abuse drugs and share a dwelling with people you don't know very well, in which case you should be taking even greater care. Or you may live at home and feel that few of the guidelines apply to you. If in doubt, get advice from a doctor or other qualified person.

• Avoid any contact with blood containing HIV and prevent this blood from entering the bloodstream. This means *never* sharing needles, syringes and other equipment used for drug abuse.

• Never handle a blood-contaminated hypodermic needle or other sharp object which has punctured the skin.

• Never have sexual intercourse with anyone known to have HIV.

• Discuss the possibility of AIDS with your sexual partner,

and follow the "safe sex" guidelines. Use a condom during intercourse.

• HIV has been detected in saliva, so deep kissing should be avoided. However, doctors have yet to report a case of the virus being passed on in this way.

• Don't become "blood brothers/sisters" by cutting the skin and mixing blood with your friends.

• Avoid tattooing.

• Only use an acupuncturist recommended by your doctor and who can satisfy you that all equipment is sterilized.

• Ear piercing – again, consider only the best clinics, and take advice from your doctor.

• Don't share razors. Skin may have been cut, leaving traces of blood on the blade or holder.

• Don't share a toothbrush. Mouth ulcers may provide a way for HIV to cross to another person. Similarly, blood from bleeding gums may also contain the virus.

Follow these safeguards, and others in this book, and those publicized on television, in papers and on posters. Then you will greatly reduce your chance of becoming infected by HIV. Try to make your friends aware, too, of the risks of passing on HIV.

Health education targeted at drug users consists of posters and leaflets in drug dependency units. It may not reach the younger, more inexperienced users, who may be most at risk. Drug Counselor.

If you've tried drugs

If you inject yourself with drugs, using equipment that has been used by an HIV-infected person, you could catch the virus yourself. You won't know at first. Once you have it, you could pass it on to other drug users if they share equipment with you. Never share your "works" with anybody, no matter how well they may seem. Don't prepare a drug with a spoon or mixing bowl used by other people. After using a needle, bend it back and dispose of it sensibly.

If you're worried because you're experimenting with drugs, the best advice is to stop. It is dangerous. Tell your doctor, or contact a local AIDS hotline or drug advice center. They may suggest a test for AIDS.

The "test for AIDS"

The "test for AIDS" is not for AIDS itself. It detects antibodies to HIV in a person's blood. If HIV antibodies are

Any process that "injects" could spread AIDS, such as tattooing.

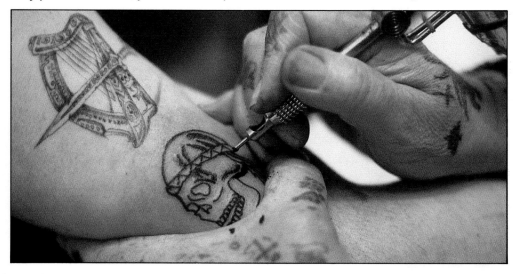

present, then the virus must be there. The result is said to be positive and the person is HIV positive.

If there are no HIV antibodies in the blood, then the result is negative. However, this does not mean for certain that HIV is absent. It can take up to three months between catching HIV and developing antibodies in the blood. If someone is tested just after infection, but before antibodies appear, then the test is negative – yet the person has HIV. For these reasons, someone at high risk of HIV infection but with a negative test result will probably be asked to take another test later. This should confirm whether antibodies have developed in the meantime.

A negative result does not give "protection." You are still at risk of becoming infected with HIV. The guidelines for avoiding AIDS should still be followed.

Taking the test

Deciding to take an AIDS test is not simple. Some versions take only a few minutes, while others take two to three weeks, before the result is known. A negative test is not proof that you are HIV-free. You may be in the "delay period" described above.

You need not go to your own doctor. In the United States, there are special clinics in main areas for sexually transmitted diseases (STDs), sometimes called venereal diseases (VDs). You can usually have a test here, and the result will be confidential.

If you are thinking of an AIDS test, it is important to get some expert advice – both before and after.

❝❝ *If someone wants to share after me, that's their business. But I'll never use a works after someone else.* ❞❞

If the test is positive

If you are told you are HIV positive, it is difficult to imagine a greater impact on your life. Counseling is vital. You will be at risk of passing HIV to others, such as your sexual partner. You may still be a drug abuser. The difficulties you may face are hard to grasp.

Of course, you can continue to work, share a home, drink and eat with your family, friends and anyone else you choose to be with. But you should alter your needle-sharing habits and sexual behavior. For women, a pregnancy may result in an HIV-infected baby.

What if you cannot give up drugs? If you have to share a needle, you must tell all the people you can that you are HIV positive. This is another difficult task, and yet another reason why expert advice from a counselor is so important.

When other people come to know that you are HIV positive, then they may well change their views on you. You may be rejected by family and friends – at first. However, attitudes are slowly changing. Often, good friends and a caring family come to understand the situation. With the right sort of expert help, and the right attitude from you,

The "AIDS test": a yellow color reveals presence of HIV antibodies.

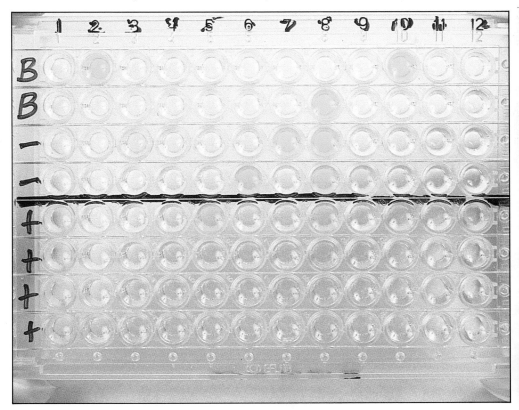

they can give help and support.

AIDS reaches into many parts of daily life. Your job and housing may be put at risk. Insurance policies and mortgages become more difficult to obtain, and perhaps more expensive. You could be breaking the rules in the small print if you do not admit you have HIV.

Some people who become infected with HIV have emotions so strong that few other people can imagine them. There is loneliness, despair, anger, frustration, regret, guilt . . . some have killed themselves, rather than face up to life on drugs and in the shadow of AIDS.

Lessons to learn

Gay communities in many countries have changed their behavior towards sex, in order to slow the spread of AIDS. Will drug injectors respond in a similar way? This is a new question. However, it seems that concern about dying from AIDS can have an effect. Most are aware that AIDS can be transmitted by sharing syringes and needles. In a New York study, this fact was known to nine out of ten drug injectors undergoing treatment. And about half of these people said they had tried to change their habits to reduce the risk of AIDS. The best change in habit would be to stop drugs altogether.

In some areas, sterile needles and syringes cannot be obtained legally. So a drug user who wants to avoid sharing has the problem of obtaining sterile equipment illegally. In Boston, street prices of clean needles doubled when the AIDS epidemic became news. In the twilight world of

Advice and counsel from an expert is important when discussing AIDS.

drug abuse, it may be illegal to obtain the drug but not the needle for injection, or the other way 'round. It depends on where you live, and whether you are signed on with a doctor or drug advice center.

Advice and help

First there was drug abuse. Agencies were set up in most regions to advise and help drug abusers. Campaigns have tried to educate people away from messing with drugs.

Then came AIDS. Who wants to know or help someone with a drug problem *and* AIDS? Yet even in these early stages, people are getting to grips with the situation. AIDS counselors and drug counselors are getting together. There are few well-established guidelines and not many well-funded organizations. In general, each city has its own organization and phone hotlines.

There is also evidence that behavior is changing. Safer sex campaigns seem to work for homosexuals. The number of new AIDS cases among homosexuals has not reached the figures predicted a few years ago. But drug abuse is now seen as the "bridge" that the virus may cross to reach the general population. Will we be able to get the message across fast enough? With AIDS and drugs, the old saying "prevention is better than cure" has never been more true. With AIDS, there is only prevention.

❝ Prevention is better than cure. And when there's no cure, prevention is all we have. ❞

Glimpses of the future

By the beginning of 1988, about 100,000 New Yorkers who injected drugs were thought to be infected with HIV. In the city, AIDS was the leading cause of death for men between 25 and 44 years of age, and for women between 25 and 34.

The figures also showed that overall in the United States, one person in four with AIDS was a drug injector. This proportion was rising. In New York City the proportion was one in three, and rising even faster.

The disease used to affect mainly "middle-class white males." Now it is spreading into the poorer parts of the city, where drug abuse is most widespread. It is affecting people of any skin color. It is affecting women – the research showed that half of the women in New York who developed

AIDS were drug injectors. And it is spreading via sex to people outside the drug community, and into the general population.

Many doctors, drug counselors and other health workers say that AIDS is a bigger threat to world health than drug abuse. They want to stop both, of course. But forced into a choice, AIDS comes first. Some experts believe that prescribing regular supplies of drugs, needles and syringes to addicts might help. It could remove one reason to share needles. It could provide addicts with a pure, controlled supply of drugs instead of the impure, risky supply from dealers. It could prevent addicts from turning to crime to pay for their habit. And it could help addicts to keep away from the criminal network of dealers and pushers.

This is a sign of how AIDS is changing some people's thinking on drug abuse, sex and many other matters. It is one point of view. But the fact is that AIDS is spreading by shared needles. Drug abuse has always been dangerous. Now AIDS has made it that much more deadly.

FACTFILE

AIDS stands for Acquired Immune Deficiency Syndrome. It is an illness that affects the immune system, which protects the body from infection by bacteria, viruses and other germs.

AIDS is caused by a virus, HIV (Human Immunodeficiency Virus). This virus spreads when blood or other body fluids mix between an infected person and a non-infected one.

Incubation period

When people are first infected with HIV, they may not realize it. There is an *incubation period* of a few months to five years or more. During this time the person looks and feels healthy, but can spread the virus to others.

The presence of HIV can be detected by the "AIDS test." This is not a test for the disease or the virus. It is a test for antibodies, substances made by the body to fight HIV. People with a positive test result have HIV antibodies in their blood and are *HIV positive*.

Full-blown AIDS

A proportion of HIV-positive people eventually develop "full-blown AIDS." This is when the virus damages their immune system, so knocking out the body's defenses against disease. Various symptoms appear (see opposite).

Not everyone with HIV develops full-blown AIDS. Statistics vary, but currently indicate that more than half of those with HIV will develop AIDS.

The time schedule

It takes up to three months after catching the virus for AIDS antibodies to develop.

The AIDS virus can incubate for years, living in the body without causing outward problems. Yet the HIV-positive person ("carrier") can pass it on to others.

AIDS in different countries

AIDS poses an enormous threat to world health. Across the globe, millions of people are HIV positive and thousands are dying from AIDS. The worst affected areas are around Central Africa. Here, AIDS is spread mainly by sex.

In the United States, there are probably one to one and a half million people infected with HIV. To March 1988, there were more than 56,000 cases of AIDS reported. Some 23,000 of these cases were reported during the past 12 months. This is an increase of almost two-fifths over the year before. Of these cases, more than two-thirds were homosexual and bisexual men. Almost one-fifth were heterosexual men and women who injected drugs.

In Japan, the drug abuse problem is smaller than in the United States. In June 1988, Japan had about 1,000 people infected with HIV. Some 80 people had AIDS, and 46 had died from it.

Drug abuse and AIDS

AIDS was first discovered in the United States in 1981, mainly in the homosexual community. In 1984 came the first confirmed reports of Aids in heterosexual drug addicts.

AIDS is carried in the blood. It was quickly found that AIDS entered the blood of drug users when they shared non-sterile needles and syringes with HIV-positive people. Sharing needles and syringes can be lethal. This is how AIDS has gained a foothold in the injecting drug community. It is spreading from here into the general population, for example by unsafe sex.

In the United States, selling needles and syringes without a prescription is illegal. There is now a growing underground industry in needles.

AIDS PROFILE

Name	AIDS (Acquired Immune Deficiency Syndrome)	*Treatments*	Some drugs can halt or slow the progression of AIDS, for a time. There is no cure and no vaccine to prevent the disease, as yet
Cause	A virus, HIV (Human Immunodeficiency Virus)		
First recognized	1981-82, in USA		
Spread	By mixing of blood and other body fluids, such as during sex, injecting using contaminated needle or syringe, injecting contaminated blood or blood products, during birth of baby to infected mother	*Those at risk*	Major types of behavior at risk are: ● injecting drug abusers; it doesn't matter which part of the body you inject, but who you share the needles and syringes with ● homosexual and bisexual men who practice anal sex ● prostitutes who inject drugs ● those who travel to areas where AIDS is more common (such as Central Africa) and have unprotected sex or share needles when injecting ● one injection is enough, you do not have to be an addict or a regular user
Incubation period	From a few months to many years, during which the infected person may look and feel well, but can spread the virus to others		
Symptoms	Develop at end of incubation period, and vary from person to person: ● loss of memory and coordination ● thrush, a white pasty growth, coats the mouth and tongue and makes it difficult to eat and swallow ● persistent diarrhea ● cancerous growths on the skin, called Kaposi's sarcoma ● cold sores on the body ● loss of weight ● lung diseases such as pneumonia ● exhaustion ● poor sleep, due to night sweats and fever ● swollen "glands" (lymph nodes)	*Containing AIDS*	"Safe sex" is one way of containing AIDS: ● use a condom correctly ● keep sexual partners to a minimum ● avoid anal sex Drug injectors can also help to contain the virus: ● stop abusing drugs ● avoid needle sharing ● always get new needles

SOURCES OF HELP

Here are some addresses and telephone numbers of organizations that can help people who are worried about AIDS and/or drug abuse.

Family doctors

Your own family doctor can give confidential advice.

AIDS Hotlines

You can call these numbers from anywhere in the United States. Calls are free and confidential, and you will get advice on where to go for help.

National Sexually Transmitted Diseases Hotline/American Social Health Association
800-227-8922

National Gay Task Force
AIDS Information Hotline
800-221-7044
(212) 807-6016 (NY State)

Information Sources

U.S. Public Health Service Public Affairs Office
Hubert H. Humphrey Building,
Room 725-H,
200 Independence Avenue S.W.,
Washington, D.C. 20201
Phone: (202) 245-6867

Local Red Cross or American Red Cross
AIDS Education Office,
1730 D Street, N.W.,
Washington, D.D. 20006
Phone: (202) 737-8300

American Association of Physicians for Human Rights
P.O. Box 14366,
San Francisco, CA94114
Phone: (415) 558-9353

AIDS Action Council
729 Eighth Street, S.E.,
Suite 200,
Washington, D.C. 20003
Phone: (202) 547-3101

Gay Men's Health Crisis
P.O. Box 274,
132 West 24th Street,
New York, NY 10011
Phone: (212) 807-6655

National AIDS Network
729 Eighth Street, S.E.,
Suite 300,
Washington, D.C. 20003
Phone: (202) 546-2424

National Association of People with AIDS
P.O. Box 65472,
Washington, D.C. 20035
Phone: (202) 483-7979

National Coalition of Gay Sexually Transmitted Disease Services
c/o Mark Behar,
P.O. Box 239,
Milwaukee, WI53201
Phone: (414) 277-7671

Minority Task Force on AIDS
c/o New York City Council of Churches
475 Riverside Drive,
Room 456,
New York, NY 10115
Phone: (212) 749-1214

Mothers of AIDS Patients (MAP)
c/o Barbara Peabody,
3403 E Street,
San Diego, CA 92102
Phone: (619) 234-3432 .

WHAT THE WORDS MEAN

AIDS Acquired Immune Deficiency Syndrome, a disease involving the body's immune system

antibody microscopic particle made by the immune system to fight and destroy invading bacteria or viruses

bisexual having sexual intercourse with members of both sexes

carrier someone who has a disease-causing "germ" in his body and who can spread it to others, but who feels no effects at the time

cell one of the millions of microscopic "building blocks" of the human body (and of all living things)

drug any chemical or other substance that changes the body's workings (including the way the person's mind works and his behavior)

drug abuse non-medical drug use with harmful effects, on the abuser and possibly on others

drug misuse using drugs in a way which people in general would see as not sensible, or not acceptable, and possibly harmful

gay homosexual

incubation period the time between a disease-causing "germ" (such as a virus) getting into the body and the period when symptoms begin to appear

heterosexual having sexual intercourse with members of the other sex

HIV Human Immunodeficiency Virus, the "germ" that causes AIDS

HIV positive having a blood test that shows antibodies to HIV (in which case the virus itself must be in the body)

homosexual having sexual intercourse with members of the same sex; also, a homosexual man

host cell a cell that plays "host" to an invading virus, enabling the virus to multiply, and being destroyed itself in the process

immune system parts of the body involved in fighting illness and destroying disease-causing viruses, bacteria and other "germs"

injection using a needle and syringe or similar equipment to break the skin and put a substance inside the body, in the blood or tissues

intravenous (i.v.) directly into a vein, usually when talking about injection

lesbian a homosexual woman

lymphocyte a type of white blood cell, that helps produce antibodies to fight illness

straight heterosexual

virus microscopic particle that invades a living cell and takes over the cell's workings in order to multiply itself, destroying the cell in the process

INDEX

Photographic Credits:
Cover: Robert Harding; pages 4, 7, 13, 15, 27, 33, 34, 39, 41 and 55:
Frank Spooner Agency; pages 9, 19, 22-23, 43 and 53: Science Photo
Library; pages 16-17: David Browne; page 25: Robert Harding Library;
pages 30 and 47: Franklin/Network; page 31: Goldwater/Network;
page 37: Rex Features; page 45: Zefa.

PRINTED IN BELGIUM BY

proost

INTERNATIONAL BOOK PRODUCTION